Jai

by Iain Gray

79 Main Street, Newtongrange,
Midlothian EH22 4NA
Tel: 0131 344 0414 Fax: 0845 075 6085
E-mail: info@lang-syne.co.uk
www.langsyneshop.co.uk

Design by Dorothy Meikle
Printed by Printwell Ltd

ISBN 978-1-85217-422-4

Jamieson

MOTTO:
It makes for the shore.

CREST:
A ship under sail.

NAME variations include:
Jameson
Jimerson
Jamesone
Jamison
Jimisone
Jamyson

The spirit of the clan means much to thousands of people

Chapter one:

The origins of the clan system

by Rennie McOwan

The original Scottish clans of the Highlands and the great families of the Lowlands and Borders were gatherings of families, relatives, allies and neighbours for mutual protection against rivals or invaders.

Scotland experienced invasion from the Vikings, the Romans and English armies from the south. The Norman invasion of what is now England also had an influence on land-holding in Scotland. Some of these invaders stayed on and in time became 'Scottish'.

The word clan derives from the Gaelic language term 'clann', meaning children, and it was first used many centuries ago as communities were formed around tribal lands in glens and mountain fastnesses.

The format of clans changed over the centuries, but at its best the chief and his family held the land on behalf of all, like trustees, and the ordinary clansmen and women believed they had a blood relationship with the founder of their clan.

There were two way duties and obligations. An inadequate chief could be deposed and replaced by someone of greater ability.

Clan people had an immense pride in race. Their relationship with the chief was like adult children to a father and they had a real dignity.

The concept of clanship is very old and a more feudal notion of authority gradually crept in.

Pictland, for instance, was divided into seven principalities ruled by feudal leaders who were the strongest and most charismatic leaders of their particular groups.

By the sixth century the 'British' kingdoms of Strathclyde, Lothian and Celtic Dalriada (Argyll) had emerged and Scotland, as one nation, began to take shape in the time of King Kenneth MacAlpin.

Some chiefs claimed descent from ancient kings which may not have been accurate in every case.

By the twelfth and thirteenth centuries the clans and families were more strongly brought under the central control of Scottish monarchs.

Lands were awarded and administered more and more under royal favour, yet the power of the area clan chiefs was still very great.

The long wars to ensure Scotland's

independence against the expansionist ideas of English monarchs extended the influence of some clans and reduced the lands of others.

Those who supported Scotland's greatest king, Robert the Bruce, were awarded the territories of the families who had opposed his claim to the Scottish throne.

In the Scottish Borders country – the notorious Debatable Lands – the great families built up a ferocious reputation for providing warlike men accustomed to raiding into England and occasionally fighting one another.

Chiefs had the power to dispense justice and to confiscate lands and clan warfare produced a society where martial virtues – courage, hardiness, tenacity – were greatly admired.

Gradually the relationship between the clans and the Crown became strained as Scottish monarchs became more orientated to life in the Lowlands and, on occasion, towards England.

The Highland clans spoke a different language, Gaelic, whereas the language of Lowland Scotland and the court was Scots and in more modern times, English.

Highlanders dressed differently, had different

customs, and their wild mountain land sometimes seemed almost foreign to people living in the Lowlands.

It must be emphasised that Gaelic culture was very rich and story-telling, poetry, piping, the clarsach (harp) and other music all flourished and were greatly respected.

Highland culture was different from other parts of Scotland but it was not inferior or less sophisticated.

Central Government, whether in London or Edinburgh, sometimes saw the Gaelic clans as a challenge to their authority and some sent expeditions into the Highlands and west to crush the power of the Lords of the Isles.

Nevertheless, when the eighteenth century Jacobite Risings came along the cause of the Stuarts was mainly supported by Highland clans.

The word Jacobite comes from the Latin for James – Jacobus. The Jacobites wanted to restore the exiled Stuarts to the throne of Britain.

The monarchies of Scotland and England became one in 1603 when King James VI of Scotland (1st of England) gained the English throne after Queen Elizabeth died.

The Union of Parliaments of Scotland and England, the Treaty of Union, took place in 1707.

Some Highland clans, of course, and Lowland families opposed the Jacobites and supported the incoming Hanoverians.

After the Jacobite cause finally went down at Culloden in 1746 a kind of ethnic cleansing took place. The power of the chiefs was curtailed. Tartan and the pipes were banned in law.

Many emigrated, some because they wanted to, some because they were evicted by force. In addition, many Highlanders left for the cities of the south to seek work.

Many of the clan lands became home to sheep and deer shooting estates.

But the warlike traditions of the clans and the great Lowland and Border families lived on, with their descendants fighting bravely for freedom in two world wars.

Remember the men from whence you came, says the Gaelic proverb, and to that could be added the role of many heroic women.

The spirit of the clan, of having roots, whether Highland or Lowland, means much to thousands of people.

Chapter two:

Kinsfolk of the clans

A name that has had resonance throughout Scotland from earliest times, 'Jamieson' is ranked at 85 in the list of the nation's 100 most common surnames.

Indicating 'son of James' or 'son of Jamie', it is to be found all over Scotland.

In Ireland, meanwhile, where the most common form is 'Jameson', many bearers are descendants of Lowland Scots who settled in the far northern province of Ulster in the seventeenth century, while the name is also an Anglicisation of the native Irish MacKeamish and MacSheamius.

While the Jamiesons of today have their own Coat of Arms, heritage and traditions, they are also recognised as septs, or sub-branches, of two Scottish clans – the Stewarts of Bute and Clan Gunn.

This identification with the Isle of Bute – a strategic point on Scotland's western seaboard – may explain the Jamieson motto of 'It makes for the shore' and crest of a ship under sail. The central motif of the Coat of Arms features three anchors.

As a sept of the Stewarts of Bute, the Jamiesons, along with others who include the Ballantynes, Hunters, MacCloys, Neilsons and Sharps, are entitled to share in the clan's heritage and traditions.

This includes the Stewart of Bute motto of 'The lion's anger is noble' and crest of a demi-lion rampant although, as noted, they also have their own proud motto and crest.

As kinsfolk of the Stewarts of Bute, the Jamiesons also shared in their fortunes and misfortunes.

Taking possession of the Lordship of Bute at the beginning of the thirteenth century, the Stewarts and their Jamieson kinsfolk were later at the forefront of Scotland's bitter and bloody Wars of Independence, fighting at the side of the great Scottish freedom fighter William Wallace.

Wallace raised the banner of revolt against the English occupation of Scotland in May of 1297, after slaying Sir William Heselrig, Sheriff of Lanark, in revenge for the killing of his young wife, Marion.

Proving an expert in the tactics of guerrilla warfare, Wallace and his hardened band of freedom fighters, who included Sir John Stewart of Bute and his kinsfolk, inflicted stunning defeats on the English garrisons.

This culminated in the liberation of practically all of Scotland following the battle of Stirling Bridge, on September 11, 1297.

Despite having a force of only 36 cavalry and 8,000 foot soldiers, compared to an army under the English Earl of Surrey that boasted no less than 200 knights and 10,000 foot soldiers, the Scots had held a strategic advantage that they exploited to the full.

Positioning their forces on the heights of the Abbey Craig, on the outskirts of Stirling, and where the imposing Wallace Monument now stands, Wallace and his army waited patiently as Essex's force slowly made its way across a narrow wooden bridge that spanned the waters of the Forth.

As the bulk of the English army crossed onto the marshy ground at the foot of the Abbey Craig, the piercing blast of a hunting horn signalled a ferocious charge down the hillside of massed ranks of Scottish spearmen.

Trapped on the boggy ground, the English were incapable of putting up any effective resistance.

They were hacked to death in their hundreds, while many others drowned in the fast-flowing waters of the Forth in their heavy armour as they attempted to make their way back across the narrow bridge.

But defeat came at the battle of Falkirk on July 22, 1298, a vicious encounter in which Sir John Stewart was killed and his clansmen and kinsfolk such as the Jamiesons all but wiped out.

But the descendants of those who survived the carnage, and those who had remained on Bute, carried on the traditions of the Stewarts and their kinsfolk.

The main seat of the clan for the past 300 years has been Mount Stuart, and it is here, on Bute, that the present Clan Chief resides.

Viking blood also flows through the blood of some bearers of the Jamieson name today, and this is because of their affiliation, as a sept, to Clan Gunn.

With their main territories in the north of Scotland, encompassing Sutherland, Caithness and the Orkney Islands, this ancient clan claims descent from Sweyn Asleifsson, also colourfully known as The Ultimate Viking.

It is through his grandson, Gunni, that the clan, whose motto is 'In peace, in war' and crest a hand clutching a sword, takes its name – with 'Gunni' an Old Norwegian word indicating 'war' or 'battle'.

The Gunns and their kinsfolk such as the Jamiesons, Robinsons, Johnsons, Williamsons and others were for centuries engaged in vicious clan warfare with their territorial rivals the Keiths.

In the much more peaceful times of the 1970s, however, representatives of both clans signed a Bond of Covenant and Friendship.

This was in 1978, symbolically bringing to an end a bitter feud whose roots lay in the dim and very distant past.

As a sept of the Gunns, who were also members of the mighty confederation of clans known as Clan Chattan, the Jamiesons are also entitled to wear their tartan.

Bearers of the Jamieson name have also gained distinction on battlefields far from their original homeland of Scotland.

Born in 1920 in Westminster, London, Major David Jamieson was a Second World War recipient of the Victoria Cross (VC), the highest award for bravery in the face of enemy action for British and Commonwealth forces.

A son of Sir Archibald Jamieson, then chairman of the British armaments company Vickers Armstrong, he had been a captain in the Royal Norfolk Regiment when, in August of 1944, following the Allied invasion of Normandy, he was in command of a company that had established a bridgehead over the River Orne.

Despite heavy enemy counter-attacks over a 36-hour period, Jamieson and his company held fast, and he was awarded the VC for the qualities of leadership and personal bravery he displayed.

Later appointed to the rank of major, he died in 2001, and his VC is now on display in the Royal Norfolk Regimental Museum, Norfolk.

Chapter three:

Buccaneering spirit

One of a noted Scottish dynasty of bearers of the name who made their mark on the historical record was the eminent Scottish naturalist and mineralogist Professor Robert Jameson, born in 1774 in Leith, on the outskirts of Edinburgh.

The son of a soap manufacturer, he studied medicine at Edinburgh University with the intention of becoming a ship's surgeon but, after having added botany, chemistry and natural history to his studies, turned his back on a career at sea.

Fascinated by geology and mineralogy, he was entrusted with charge of the university's natural history collection, while he also carried out extensive geological fieldwork in the Hebrides, Orkney, the Shetland Islands, the west coast Scottish island of Arran and on the Irish mainland.

It was in recognition of his natural history expertise that, in 1804, he was appointed Edinburgh University's Regius Professor of Natural History – a post that he held with distinction up until his death in 1854.

As a professor, one of his pupils was a young Charles Darwin, later to make his own distinguished name in the field of natural history.

The author of several books that included his 1880 *Mineralogy of the Scottish Isles*, Jameson also helped to build up an impressive collection of geological and mineralogical specimens for the university museum – later transferred to what is now Scotland's Royal Museum in Edinburgh.

One of his nephews was the playwright, poet and newspaper editor Robert William Jameson, born in Edinburgh in 1805.

A son of the wealthy ship owner and merchant Thomas Jameson, it was through his interest in journalism that his friend and patron the Earl of Stair made him editor of his newspaper *The Wigtownshire Free Press*, based in Stranraer, in the southwest of Scotland.

In addition to his newspaper work, he also penned a number of poems, including *Nimrod* and, inspired by the anti-slavery sentiments of his time, the play *Timolean*.

He was the father of the controversial medical doctor, colonial administrator and politician Sir Leander Starr Jameson, whose life and times are as colourful and dramatic as the circumstances under which he came to obtain his name in the first place.

His father had been nervously pacing the banks of a heavily swollen stream near his home in Stranraer, anxiously awaiting the birth of his son, when he stumbled and fell into the water.

Fortunately, an American visitor to Scotland who had been walking nearby observed his plight and, plunging into the stream, rescued him.

His son was born only a short time later, and it was in gratitude to the American stranger – Leander Starr – that Jameson made him his son's godfather and named the child Leander Starr Jameson.

Born in 1854 and the youngest of twelve children, Jameson studied medicine at University College Hospital, London, later qualifying as a doctor.

Appointed a resident medical officer at the hospital, his health broke down from overwork and he left British shores for South Africa, setting up a medical practice at Kimberley in 1878. His practice thrived, and one of his many patients was Lobengula, Chief of the Matabele tribe, and Jameson used his influence with him to persuade him to grant valuable land concessions to his friend Cecil Rhodes, later head of the South Africa Company and Prime Minister of Cape Colony.

Abandoning his medical practice, Jameson joined an expedition into Mashonaland in 1890, and his buccaneering spirit led him five years later to recruit a private army on behalf of Rhodes in an attempt to overthrow the Boer government of the Transvaal.

This was at a time when he held the post of Administrator General for Matabeleland.

In the infamous Jameson Raid of December 1895, Jameson's army of adventurers reached within 20 miles of Johannesburg before being defeated and its leaders, including Jameson, captured.

The raid had been launched without official British government sanction and Jameson, handed over to the British authorities by the Boers, was put on trial in London in February of the following year.

Found guilty of having breached agreements that Britain had made with the Boers, he was sentenced to fifteen months imprisonment.

But, despite the failure of the Jameson Raid, he had become a public hero in Britain and the government, using his ill health as an excuse, pardoned him shortly after the trial.

Returning to South Africa, he became leader of the Progressive (British) Party in Cape Colony, serving as Prime Minister of the colony from 1904 to 1908.

His fortunes and influence still in the ascendant, he also served from 1910 to 1912 as leader of the Unionist Party (South Africa).

The British government had forgiven him his past transgressions and, accordingly, created him a baronet in 1911.

Jameson returned to England in 1912, and it was here that he died five years later.

He was buried in London, but his body was taken back to South Africa in 1920 and re-interred in a grave on the top of a hill in Matobo National Park, south of Bulawayo, the hill having once been described by his great friend Rhodes – who subsequently gave his name to Rhodesia, now Zimbabwe – as "The View of the World."

The National Portrait Gallery in London holds three portraits of Jameson.

One was executed by his older brother, the artist Middleton Jameson, and another by fellow Scottish painter David Octavius Hill.

Rudyard Kipling's famous poem *If* was written, according to Kipling himself, in celebration of Jameson's personal qualities in overcoming the difficulties that followed him after the failed raid.

In a much different field of endeavour, John

Jamieson was the Church of Scotland minister, antiquarian and lexicographer renowned for his exhaustive two-volume *Etymological Dictionary of the Scottish Language*, compiled between 1808 and 1825.

Born in 1759 in Glasgow, the son of a minister, his dictionary remained the definitive work on the Scottish language until the publication in 1931 of the *Scottish National Dictionary*, which drew heavily on his work.

Honoured with distinctions that included fellowships of the Society of Antiquaries of Scotland, the American Antiquarian Society and the Royal Society of America, he died in 1838.

Yet another noted antiquary was Robert Jamieson, responsible for the publication at the age of 26 of a collection of nearly 150 traditional Scottish ballads and songs.

Born in 1780 in Morayshire, he died in 1844.

From ballads and songs to the liquor trade, John Jameson was the Scottish lawyer who founded the Jameson Whiskey Company.

Born in Alloa in 1740, he married Margaret Haig, a sister of the brothers who had founded the Haig Scotch Whisky Company.

The Haigs were related to another Scotch

whisky family, the Steins, who also had business interests in Dublin – and it was here that John Jameson, along with his son John, established the firm of John Jameson in 1780.

Originally produced from a distillery in Bow Street, Jameson Whiskey is now distilled in Cork, although still vatted in Dublin.

Now produced by a division of the French distiller Pernod Ricard, it is recognised as the best-selling Irish whiskey in the world.

r:

e world stage

l in Worcestershire, Susan Jameson is a actress who has had roles in several evision soaps and series that include ***n Street, Holby City, Take Three Girls, Dalziel and Pascoe*** **and, along with her husband the actor James Bolam,** ***When the Boat Comes In.***

Also known for her work as an audio book narrator, particularly of Catherine Cookson novels, in 2009 she was one of five actresses who portrayed the Queen at various stages in her life in the Channel 4 series *The Queen*.

Also on British television screens, **Louise Jameson**, born in 1951 in Wanstead, London is the actress who, after having spent some time with the Royal Shakespeare Company, has had roles in television soaps and series that include *Bergerac*, *Emmerdale*, *EastEnders* and *River City*.

It was Jameson, through her charitable work as a prison visitor, who met Leslie Grantham in the early 1970s while he was serving 12 years of a life sentence for murder.

She encouraged him to take up acting on his release, and in 1985 he secured the memorable role of Den Watts in *EastEnders*.

Although born in 1920 in Evanston, Illinois, **James Jamieson**, also known as Jamie Jamieson, was the American dancer and choreographer recognised as a specialist in Scottish Highland dancing.

An internationally recognised champion of traditional Scottish dance, he was chosen to coach the cast in Scottish dancing for the 1954 film *Brigadoon*; he died in 1993.

President of the Canadian Association of Broadcasting from 1961 to 1964, **Donald Jamieson**, born in 1921 in St John's, Newfoundland, was the broadcaster, diplomat and politician whose paternal grandfather was a fisherman who had settled in Newfoundland from Scotland.

Reporting from the Parliament of Canada in 1945 on the negotiations that led to Newfoundland being invited to join the Canadian Confederation, he later established both a privately operated radio network in Newfoundland and CJON-TV, the island's first television station.

Entering politics in 1966 for the Liberal Party of Canada, he later served in a number of government posts that included Minister of Defence Production and Secretary of State for External Affairs, while from 1982 until a year before his death in 1986, as Canada's High Commissioner to the United Kingdom.

In the creative world of art, **George Jamesone**, born in about 1587 in Aberdeen, the son of a stone-mason, is recognised today as Scotland's first eminent portrait painter.

He first came to attention for his portraits of Aberdeen worthies, but achieved much wider fame in 1638 when he executed a portrait of Charles I when the monarch visited Edinburgh.

Charles was so pleased with the portrait that he gifted Jamesone with a ring from his finger as a reward.

This royal seal of approval led to commissions from much of the Scottish gentry of his day.

He died in 1644, while his self-portrait now graces the National Gallery of Scotland, Edinburgh.

In the equally creative world of architecture, **James Paterson Jamieson**, born in Falkirk in 1867 and who died in 1941, was the Scottish architect who, after studying at the School of the South Kensington Museum, London, immigrated to the United States.

By 1912 he had set up his own architectural

practice in St Louis, Missouri, and was joined six years later by fellow Scots architect George Spearl.

The partners went on to design most of the buildings for the University of Missouri and Washington University, St Louis.

From art and architecture to the highly competitive world of sport, **Jane Jamieson**, born in 1975, is the Australian track and field athlete who won the gold medal for the heptathlon at the 2002 Commonwealth Games in Manchester, while on the golf course **James A. Jamieson** was a leading American golfer of the early 1970s.

Born in 1943 in Kalamazoo, Michigan, he had, between 1971 and 1973, four top-six finishes in major championships, winning the Western Open in 1972.

Also on the golf course, **Betty Jameson**, born in 1919 in Norman, Oklahoma was the American professional golfer, who, in 1950, was one of the founders of the Ladies Professional Golf Association (LPGA).

Winner of the United States Women's Amateur Golf Championship in 1939 and 1940, she turned professional in 1945, winning the U.S. Women's Open in 1947 and the LPGA Championship in 1956 and 1958. An inductee of the World Golf Hall of Fame, she died in 2009.

In the Canadian national sport of ice hockey, **Jim Jamieson**, born in 1922 in Brantford, Ontario is the retired defence-man who played in the National Hockey League (NHL) for the New York Rangers during the 1943-1944 NHL season.

On the fields of European football, **Scott Jamieson**, born in 1988 in Auburn, New South Wales is the Australian left back and left winger who, in addition to playing for his national team, has also played for English team Bolton Wanderers.

Also from Australia, but from football to the cerebral world of chess, **Robert Jamieson** is the International Master who was born in 1952.

Winner of the Australian Championship in 1974 and 1978, and having played in five Chess Olympiads between 1974 and 1982, he established an Australian 'simultaneous' record in 1975 by playing 145 opponents at the same time.

In baseball, **Charles Jamieson**, born in 1893 in Paterson, New Jersey, and nicknamed "Cuckoo", was the talented outfielder who, between 1915 and 1932, played for The Washington Senators, Philadelphia Athletics and Cleveland Indians; he died in 1969.

From sport to music, **Phil Jamieson**, born in 1977 in Wauchope, New South Wales, is the founder of the Australian rock band Grinspoon, while **Reid Jamieson**, born in 1973 in Toronto, is the Canadian singer and songwriter whose best-selling albums include his 2004 *The Unavoidable Truth* and the 2010 *The Staring Contest*.

In the ecclesiastical realm, **Penelope Jamieson** is the second woman in the world to have held the appointment of bishop in the Anglican Church.

Born in 1942 in Chalfont St Giles, Buckinghamshire, she studied linguistics at Edinburgh University before settling in New Zealand, the land of her husband's birth.

Ordained to the Anglican priesthood in 1985, she was appointed curate of St James' Lower Hutt and later vicar of Karori West, in the Diocese of Wellington.

Despite some male opposition from within the Church at the time, she was appointed seventh Bishop of Dunedin in 1989, serving in the post until her retirement in 2004.

In the world of the written word, Margaret Storm Jameson, better known as **Storm Jameson**, was the prolific English writer who was born in 1891 in Whitby, Yorkshire.

A prominent member of the British branch of

the International PEN Association and active in helping refugee writers, her many books include the 1919 *The Pot Boils*, the 1941 *The End of This War* and, published thirteen years before her death in 1986, *There Will Be a Short Interval*.

In the futuristic world of science fiction, **Malcolm Jameson** was both an officer in the United States Navy and a writer of stories for American pulp magazines.

Born in 1891, his 1941 tale *Doubled and Redoubled* is considered to be among the first to use the theme of a time loop.

Other stories include his 1942 *The Old Ones Hear* and, published two years before his death in 1945, *The Blind Alley*.

In the world of journalism, **Derek Jameson** is the retired British tabloid journalist and radio broadcaster who was born in 1929 in London.

Beginning his newspaper career as a messenger boy in London's Fleet Street, he later gained prominence as editor of the *Daily Express*, *Daily Star* and *News of the World*, and as managing editor of the *Daily Mirror*.

Joining BBC Radio 2 in 1985, he was host of the station's breakfast show from 1986 to 1991, while for a time he also hosted a late-night show along with his wife, Ellen.

Executive Editor of the "Scotsman" Newspaper, **Bill Jamieson** is the veteran Scottish journalist who writes on politics, current affairs, finance and ecconomics.

Winner of the Business Journalist of the Year Award at the 2009 Scottish Press Awards, he is also the author of a number of books that include *An Illustrated Guide to the Brittish Economy*.

From journalism to medicine, **James Jamieson**, born in 1840 in Beith, Ayrshire, and who died in 1916, was the prominent Scots-born Australian doctor who contributed to a number of important medical publications, including the *Medical Journal of Australia*, and of which he was editor from 1883 to 1887.

Educated at Glasgow University, he immigrated to Australia and set up a medical practice in 1868 in Warrnambool, later moving to Melbourne and lecturing at Melbourne University.

In the legal world, Douglas Jamieson, appointed to Scotland's Court of Session with the judicial title of **Lord Jamieson**, was a leading Unionist politician and judge. Born in 1880, he also served as Solicitor General for Scotland and as Lord Advocate; he died in 1952.

In contemporary Scottish politics, **Cathy Jamieson**, born in 1956 in Kilmarnock, East Ayrshire is the Scottish Labour politician who has served as a Member of the Scottish Parliament (MSP) for Carrick, Cumnock and Doon Valley.

Also having held posts that include Minister for Justice and Shadow Secretary for Health and Well-being, in 2010 she was also elected Member of Parliament (MP) in the Westminster Parliament for Kilmarnock and Loudon.

Also born in Kilmarnock, three years before Cathy Jamieson, **Margaret Jamieson** is the Scottish Labour politician who served as MSP for Kilmarnock and Loudon from 1999 to 2007.

From Scottish to Canadian politics, **Reuben Jamieson**, born in 1856 in Westover, Ontario, served from 1909 until shortly before his death in 1911 as 16th Mayor of Calgary, Alberta.

His wife, **Alice Jamieson**, was active in the struggle for voting rights for women and, in 1914, was appointed as the first juvenile court judge in the British Empire, later becoming magistrate of Calgary's women's court.

Born of Scottish ancestry in 1923 in Perth, Western Australia, **Colin Jamieson** was the veteran Australian Labor Party politician who served as a member of the Western Australian Legislative Assembly from 1953 until four years before his death in 1990.

His grandfather, **Archibald "Scottie" Jamieson**, who immigrated to Australia from the Orkney Islands, was instrumental in the foundation of the Midland Railway Workers Union, and also served from 1914 to 1915 as Mayor of Midland Junction Municipality.

Recognised as one of America's leading experts on political campaigning and advertising, **Kathleen Jamieson**, born in 1946, is the author of books that include her 1984 *Packaging the Presidency* and co-author of the 2010 *The Obama Victory: How Money, Media and Messages Shaped the 2008 Election*.

The proud name of Jamieson also survives on the landscape, including in the form of the river and the town of Jamieson, in Victoria, Australia.

Both are named in honour of **George Jamieson**, a shepherd who grazed his flock in the area in the 1850s.